Effective Listening Skills

Effective Listening Skills

DENNIS M. KRATZ, Ph.D.
ABBY ROBINSON KRATZ, Ed.M.
in cooperation with Art James Productions, Inc.

Business Skills Express Series

IRWIN
Professional Publishing

MIRROR PRESS
Chicago • Bogotá • Boston • Buenos Aires • Caracas
London • Madrid • Mexico City • Sydney • Toronto

IRWIN
Concerned About Our Environment

In recognition of the fact that our company is a large end-user of
fragile yet replenishable resources, we at IRWIN can assure you
that every effort is made to meet or exceed Environmental Protection Agency
(EPA) recommendations and requirements for a "greener" workplace.

To preserve these natural assets, a number of environmental policies, both
companywide and department-specific, have been implemented. From the
use of 50% recycled paper in our textbooks to the printing of promotional
materials with recycled stock and soy inks to our office paper recycling program, we are committed to reducing waste and replacing environmentally
unsafe products with safer alternatives.

© Richard D. Irwin, Inc., 1995

Mirror Press:	David R. Helmstadter
	Carla F. Tishler
Editor in chief:	Jeffrey A. Krames
Project editor:	Paula M. Buschman
Production supervisor:	Pat Frederickson
Designer:	Laurie J. Entringer
Compositor:	Alexander Graphics, Ltd.
Typeface:	12/14 Criterion Book
Printer:	Malloy Lithographing, Inc.

Library of Congress Cataloging-in-Publication Data

Kratz, Dennis M.
     Effective listening skills/Dennis M. Kratz, Abby Robinson Kratz
   ; in cooperation with Art James Productions, Inc.
        p.   cm.—(Business skills express series)
     ISBN 0-7863-0122-8
     1. Communication in business.   2. Listening.   3. Interpersonal
communication.   I. Kratz, Abby Robinson.   II. Art James
Productions.   III. Title.   IV. Series.
HF5718.K72   1995
658.4'52—dc20   94–44688

Printed in the United States of America
1 2 3 4 5 6 7 8 9 0 ML 2 1 0 9 8 7 6 5

PREFACE

The fact that you have picked up this book indicates that you already have given some thought to improving your skills as a listener. Now you may be wondering what to expect from the book. Will reading it make you a more effective listener? What are the basic principles behind the book?

Imagine the following situation:

Jack and Bridget Reilly are about to leave on a vacation. The bags are packed. The car is filled with gas.

They pull onto the highway. Jack turns to his wife and asks her to look at the road map and figure out the best route to their destination.

"There's only one problem," she replies. "You haven't told me where we are going."

"Oh," he says, "I don't have any place picked out. But I do want to get there as quickly as possible." ■

Sound absurd? Of course it does. How can we decide the best way to get someplace if we don't know where we are going?

Listening is often like driving. This book might even be described as a kind of driver's instruction book for listeners. We present some basic, general principles and a number of specific examples, but the rest is up to you. You can't improve your driving without practice, and you can't improve your listening merely by reading a book. You will have to perform the prescribed exercises in the book and practice them in your everyday conversations.

Think of your current listening skills in the same way as your driving skills. First, is your vehicle well maintained? Or have you neglected it? Have you checked directions or maps, weather reports, and traffic reports? Are there any driving problems that have caused you trouble in the past? You may drive differently, and take different routes, depending on the situation and the reasons for your traveling.

Just as your driving depends on the situation, listening to a friend talk about a vacation and listening to a sales pitch also require different approaches. Different listening situations call for different skills and approaches.

We have written this book with one main objective: to help you become a more effective listener. By *effective* we mean able to recognize different listening situations and apply appropriate skills to each situation.

The Golden Rule of Listening

All the principles and all the exercises presented in this book can be expressed in one basic rule of effective listening. The Golden Rule of listening is simple and clear:

Listen to others as you would like others to listen to you.

Keep this rule in mind throughout the book. When you are trying to explain something, what kind of listener do you want? When you are trying to sell an idea (or a product), how would you like the other person to listen? When you are upset or have good news to share, what kind of listener do you want?

This book will help you do more than imagine the kind of listening you would like to receive when you are talking. It will help you become that kind of listener to others.

Dennis Kratz
Abby Kratz

ABOUT THE AUTHORS

Dennis M. Kratz, Ph.D., is Dean of Undergraduate Studies at the University of Texas at Dallas. He is also a Professor at UT, Dallas, and Co-Director of the Center for Translation Studies there. Dr. Kratz is a widely published author of books and numerous articles on medieval and epic literature and an experienced international speaker. He received his Ph.D. and M.A. at Harvard University.

Abby Robinson Kratz, Ed.M., is a librarian at the University of Texas at Dallas, and she has a broad background in library science. In addition, she has taught at the university level. Ms. Kratz is an active member of the American Library Association and related professional associations. She earned her Ed.M. from Harvard University.

About Art James Productions, Inc.

Close to 200 of America's most successful companies have employed Art James Productions' educational programs to entertain and inform their personnel. These programs range from TV-style game shows to computer-based interactive multimedia learning—all devoted to strengthening professional and interpersonal skills, including listening, one of the most essential elements in any human transaction. For more information about Art James Productions, Inc., contact:

Art James Productions, Inc.
9580 Laketown Rd.
Chaska, MN 55318
(612) 442-1634

ABOUT IRWIN PROFESSIONAL PUBLISHING

Irwin Professional Publishing is the nation's premier publisher of business books. As a Times Mirror company, we work closely with Times Mirror training organizations, including Zenger-Miller, Inc.; Learning International, Inc.; and Kaset International to serve the training needs of business and industry.

About the Business Skills Express Series

This expanding series of authoritative, concise, and fast-paced books delivers high-quality training on key business topics at a remarkably affordable cost. The series will help managers, supervisors, and frontline personnel in organizations of all sizes and types hone their business skills while enhancing job performance and career satisfaction.

Business Skills Express books are ideal for employee seminars, independent self-study, on-the-job training, and classroom-based instruction. Express books are also convenient-to-use references at work.

CONTENTS

Preface
v

Self-Assessment
xv

Chapter 1   1
The Basics of Listening
What Is Listening? 2
Why Is Listening Important? 3
Building a Communication Model 4
Three Principles of Communication 8
A Four-Phase Model of Listening 8
Five Types of Listening 10

Chapter 2   19
Giving and Getting Feedback
What Is Feedback? 20
Rethinking the Model 21
Feedback without Words 21
Directive Feedback 24
Nondirective Feedback 25
Using Questions as Feedback 27
Why Ask Questions? 30

Chapter 3   33
Noise Pollution
What Is Noise? 34
External Noise 34
Internal Noise 37

Chapter 4   **45**
Listening to Learn

Listening for Information   46

Formal and Informal Listening   48

Reaching Your Goal   49

A Learning Attitude   50

Note Taking   52

Listening Is Interactive   55

Do You Listen as You Talk?   56

Chapter 5   **61**
Listening to Decide

Understanding before Deciding   62

Assertions and Claims   62

Fair Play or Manipulation?   65

Warning Signs   66

The Structure of Persuasion   71

Remember: The Listener Decides   73

Chapter 6   **75**
Listening to Enable

What Is Empathy?   76

Emotions Equal Messages   77

Two Big Don'ts   78

Keep Your Goal in Mind   78

Affirm, Understand, Endorse, Enable   79

Listening to Emotions   84

Using Your Knowledge   85

A Final Note   88

Post-Test   **90**

Self-Assessment

Effective listening skills are crucial to successful communication in the workplace, with family and friends, and in every situation where messages are sent and received. Use the self-assessment below to measure your current level of listening expertise. The chapters in *Effective Listening Skills* will help you build on your current skills and hone new ones. Good luck!

	Almost Always	Sometimes	Almost Never
1. In a conversation, I am able to interpret and evaluate others' comments, going beyond the surface meaning of words.	_____	_____	_____
2. I am able to adapt my listening skills to fit different requirements of a listening situation.	_____	_____	_____
3. I can differentiate between the five functions of communication and listen and respond accordingly.	_____	_____	_____
4. I use feedback effectively to elicit honest and direct communication from others.	_____	_____	_____
5. I screen out noise and outside distractions to concentrate on speakers' messages.	_____	_____	_____
6. I recognize and eliminate inner distractions to better focus on speakers.	_____	_____	_____
7. I listen for content rather than style.	_____	_____	_____
8. I adopt and practice a ready-to-learn attitude when listening to others.	_____	_____	_____
9. I practice a concise and reliable system of note-taking.	_____	_____	_____
10. I am a critical listener, able to discern assertions from facts.	_____	_____	_____
11. I listen empathically, enabling others to express their emotions in a nonthreatening atmosphere.	_____	_____	_____
12. I enable people to move from feelings to positive action by helping them set and meet goals.	_____	_____	_____

1 | The Basics of Listening

This chapter will help you to:

- Define listening.
- Relate listening to the process of communication.
- Understand the four stages of the listening process.
- Identify five types of listening.

Anna Rivera was already running late that morning when she heard on the radio that it was supposed to rain heavily. Anna decided to leave for work as early as possible since traffic conditions would be terrible. But at breakfast her daughter's tone of voice indicated that Jennie was upset, and Anna wanted to talk with her until Jennie felt better.

Driving to work, Anna listened to the news but was concerned by a knocking sound in her car's engine. "Time for a tune-up," she thought.

As she walked into her office, the phone was ringing. It was her supervisor, calling a staff meeting for eleven o'clock. Before the meeting, Anna interviewed an applicant for the new job in merchandising and also talked with a representative who tried to persuade her to switch long-distance telephone plans.

1

She was on her way to the staff meeting when Bill Roberts, one of her assistants, stopped to ask her advice. Because she was late for the meeting, Anna asked Bill to come by her office that afternoon.

At the staff meeting an outside consultant gave a presentation on the importance of effective listening in management. Anna did not have to be convinced. ■

WHAT IS LISTENING?

Listening is the act by which we *make sense of sounds.* The most common form of listening involves *spoken messages.* Anna Rivera listened to individuals in a wide range of situations—in person, on the telephone, and on the radio.

However, the act of listening is not limited to language or even to people. We make sense out of other sounds as well. A doctor, for example, can learn about the state of a patient's health by listening to that person's breathing or heartbeat. A skilled mechanic can identify a problem by listening to a running engine.

Time Out

1. What sounds did Anna Rivera listen to that did not involve spoken messages?

    a. _____

    b. _____

2. When did Anna make an interpretation based on something more than the words she heard?

    _____

3. When did Anna participate in each of the following types of listening situations?

    a. Listening to someone primarily for information.

    _____

    _____

    b. Listening to someone with a problem.

    _____

    _____

    c. Listening to someone trying to persuade her to take a specific course of action.

    _____

    _____

Check Your Answers

1. *a.* The noise in her engine.
    b. The ringing telephone.

2.   Her daughter's tone of voice.

3. *a.* The news on the radio; listening to her supervisor.
    b. Her daughter; Bill Roberts.
    c. The job applicant; the sales representative.

WHY IS LISTENING IMPORTANT?

Studies reveal that most people spend as much as 90 percent of their working days in one of the four modes of communication: writing, reading, speaking, and listening. Of these four modes, however, we devote *more than half* our time to listening. We spend about 30 percent of our time listening to mass communication media (radio, television) and 25 percent listening to other people (either in person or on the telephone). Moreover, research shows that individuals in managerial positions spend even more time listening—as much as 70 percent of the typical day. The higher the position, the more time is spent listening to others. It is not surprising then that effective listening is regarded as one of the most important skills for a manager to possess.

1

■ Think about It

The fact that you are reading this book indicates that you already recognize the importance of listening and perhaps are concerned with the quality of your listening skills. On the lines below list five work-related activities that involve listening. Rate yourself on a scale of 1 to 5 (with 1 being "poor" and 5 "outstanding") as a listener in each situation. If your grade is less than perfect, briefly describe why you are dissatisfied with your performance.

SITUATION	GRADE	COMMENTS
1. _____	_____	_____
2. _____	_____	_____
3. _____	_____	_____
4. _____	_____	_____
5. _____	_____	_____

Although many people take listening for granted, it is a complex skill that can be improved with training. Let your list of dissatisfactions serve as a starting point to improve yourself as a listener. The first step in this program of improvement is to understand the nature of listening as a part of the larger process of communication.

BUILDING A COMMUNICATION MODEL

Communication is the process by which one person sends a message to another. This process has four primary elements:

1. The sender
2. The message
3. The channel of communication
4. The receiver

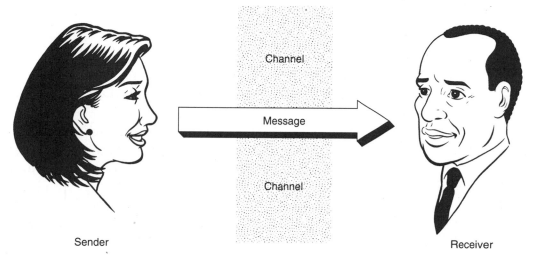

A Communication Model.

The Sender

The process begins when an individual, called the *sender*, has something to communicate. The sender may want to impart some information to another person or encourage that person to do something.

The Message

Let's go back to Anna Rivera in her office. Suppose Anna wants her secretary to locate a file concerning an important account. Since Anna cannot expect her secretary to read her mind, she must translate her wish into a message that her secretary will understand. This act of translating is often called *encoding*. Anna has become the sender and "Bring me the Perkins file" has become the message.

The Channel of Communication

Note that senders have numerous choices when it comes to encoding, that is, translating wishes into messages. They can use words, for example.

1

If they decide to use words, they can either speak or write a note. Or they can depend on a gesture to communicate meaning. The chosen medium is called the *channel of communication.*

Spoken language is a channel of communication. *How* people say those words, however, can be as important as the words themselves.

All speakers use vocal signals that affect the meaning of words. How loudly they speak, what words are stressed, the tempo of speech—all these elements that we call the speaker's tone of voice—determine the message.

The Receiver

When the message reaches the receiver, in this case Anna's secretary, the basic process we just described occurs in reverse. The receiver must try to understand from the message what the sender was trying to express. The receiver's role in the process is to *decode* the message.

The role of the receiver in this process has four phases:

1. *Sense:* The receiver becomes aware of the message.
2. *Interpret:* The receiver tries to understand the meaning and purpose of the message.
3. *Evaluate:* The receiver decides whether the message is important (worth responding to or acting on).
4. *Respond:* The receiver responds to the message by acting or by sending another message.

In this simple example, Anna's secretary receives the message, undertands that Anna wants the Perkins file, and acts on this interpretation by bringing the file to her. The communication has been successful.

1

■ Time Out

In the following exercise, you are the *sender.* You are at a concert, and you want the person sitting next to you to stop talking so that you can hear. Translate the *message* in the following ways:

1. Use words politely.
2. Use the same words but in a tone expressing annoyance.
3. Use sounds, not words, politely.
4. Use a polite gesture.
5. Use a combination of words and a gesture to express annoyance.

Think about Your Answers

In an exercise like this, there are no "right" or "wrong" answers, and you might want to try out your responses on someone else. Let that person tell you if you are expressing what you intend. Here are some possible responses:

1. "Would you please stop talking?"
2. "Would you *please* stop talking!"
3. Here you might use a subdued cough. What sounds do you make to indicate politely that someone is annoying you?
4. A finger to your lips while smiling might work in such a situation.
5. Here you might try to combine some of the previous answers.

This basic model of communication holds true whatever the channel of communication. In many ways listening is more challenging than reading. Think about it. Unless you are listening to a recorded speech, for example, you will not have the opportunity to reread what is being presented. Moreover, spoken messages make use of more than words. You have to consider such elements as tone of voice and inflection in interpreting the speaker's meaning. Finally, when you can *see* the person who is speaking, you have to take into account gestures and other forms of nonverbal communication.

THREE PRINCIPLES OF COMMUNICATION

If there is one basic principle that you need to remember about communication, this is it: *Communication is a system.* It takes at least two people for communication to happen. The receiver *shares responsibility* with the sender for the message to get through.

Here is a second principle to keep in mind: *It is impossible not to communicate.* Whenever two or more people are interacting, messages are being sent and received. It is human nature to create and interpret meaning. Even if you are not talking, the other person will be interpreting your facial expressions, gestures, and other behavior. Indeed, many of the messages we send are unintentional.

This fact brings us to a third basic principle: *It is impossible to predict or control the interpretation of a message.* No two people have the exact same history, personality, or perspective. Recent studies have shown, for example, that women and men use and respond to language differently. Moreover, different cultures, even within the same country, have different attitudes toward what consitutes proper language.

A FOUR-PHASE MODEL OF LISTENING

Listening involves four phases: sensing, interpreting, evaluating, and responding.

Sensing

The first stage in the listening process occurs when sound waves reach our ears, and we become aware that someone is trying to communicate with us. It is important to realize that we hear only a small portion of the sounds that literally bombard us every waking moment. Our brains filter out many of these sounds before they reach our conscious awareness.

We need to emphasize the distinction between sensing and listening. By *sensing* we mean the physical reception of sounds. By *listening* we

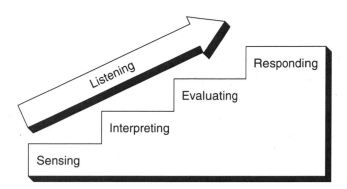

mean the four-phase mental process of understanding and interpreting the sounds that we hear in order to respond appropriately.

Interpreting

In this stage we assign meaning and importance to the sounds that we hear. For example, if we hear bells ringing at a railroad crossing, we make the following interpretation: "The bells are warning me to stop for an oncoming train." When we hear someone talking, we listen for cues to the meaning of the words. Suppose Anna's immediate supervisor says, "You might want to take a look at this report before the meeting." Anna has to interpret this statement, taking into account her supervisor's tone. Presumably she will interpret the phrase "might want to" as meaning "it would be a very good idea" to read that report.

Evaluating

Our evaluation of a message and response to it are intimately related. Evaluating means determining the importance of the message we have just heard. Do I believe what I have heard? Should I take action as a result of this message?

1

Responding

The action we take as a result of the message is our response. If we choose *not* to act as a result, then our response is to ignore the message. If we choose not to ignore the message, then the question becomes, What action should I take as a result of this message? If I decide that the imminent arrival of a train is not particularly important, I can ignore the message. My response will be to continue driving (at least for a little while longer). If I believe the message is telling me something important, then I will respond by stopping the car.

When Anna Rivera heard the forecast of rain, she responded by changing her behavior. She left for work (or tried to) earlier than usual. Perhaps she also dressed differently and took an umbrella. Anna interpreted the noise in her car's engine as an indication of a possible problem. Her evaluation of the potential seriousness of this problem will affect her response.

FIVE TYPES OF LISTENING

In general, people send messages, or communicate, for one of five reasons. As you will see, each reason results in a slightly different kind of message and therefore requires a slightly different kind of listening. Although the five types of messages are distinct, they are not exclusive. In fact, most of our conversations are composed of at least two and sometimes all five modes.

1. Social Contact: Listening to Bond

One important reason why we communicate is simply to make contact with or express our friendship for another person. Conversations between friends and family members often have more to do with building or strengthening a relationship than with imparting information about a specific subject. When we say, "How are you today?" to a friend, we are not really expecting a medical report. Jokes and casual conversations

1

about such everyday subjects as the weather or sports are ways of expressing our friendship with another person.

Since the information that we receive in this situation is less important than the fact that we are strengthening or establishing a relationship, social listening calls for a less critical and more appreciative perspective. We are *listening in order to bond.*

2. Entertainment: Listening to Appreciate

Some of the time we listen primarily for enjoyment. We go to concerts and the theater. We listen to music on tape or on a CD. For the most part we are *listening to appreciate* rather than to evaluate or analyze.

3. Information: Listening to Learn

The third reason we send a message is to share information. This form of communication takes place when we give directions or explain something to another person. In this situation we *listen in order to learn* and retain information. We assume that the main purpose of the speaker is to transmit an idea or information to us. Since we are listening to learn, our primary goal is to understand what the other person has to say rather than to criticize or judge it.

4. Persuasion: Listening to Decide

We also communicate to persuade another person to do something: to move closer, to write a report, to buy a product. Advertising provides an obvious example of persuasive communication. If you think about it, you will find that most communication is at least partly persuasive. After all, we want others to accept our views and us.

When the message is persuasive, we need to listen critically. We assume that the speaker is trying to persuade us rather than merely to share ideas. Our goal is to discover the validity (or the weaknesses) of

1

arguments that are being presented. We listen critically to a salesperson trying to persuade us to buy something, to a political candidate seeking our vote, and to a potential employee presenting a case for hiring her. In essence, we are *listening in order to decide*.

5. Catharsis: Listening to Enable

A fifth reason to communicate is to "get something off our chest." This type of communication, called cathartic, usually takes place when the speaker has a problem or is experiencing frustration. Its primary goal is to vent a particular emotion or feeling.

We realize that the speaker is trying to communicate feelings more than ideas. The speaker does not want us to judge or criticize what is being said. We realize that we are expected to be understanding, accepting, and empathic (that is, we imagine how we would feel in that person's situation). Empathic listening, then, is similar to both social and informational listening. In both cases we are listening to understand. The main differences lie in the kind of information to which the listener is attentive, and in the fact that, in empathetic situations, we are *listening in order to enable* the other person to express strong feelings and perhaps find a solution to the problem that has evoked those feelings.

Review What You Have Learned

For each of the following statements identify (1) the type of message and (2) the kind of listening required. Be careful! It is possible that you will find more than one reason for the message that is being expressed:

1. "What a lovely house you have," said the insurance salesman to the O'Keefes.
   Message: _____
   Listening: _____

2. "You're blind, ump! He missed the tag!"
   Message: _____
   Listening: _____

3. "How are you today?" Tom asked his friend Jed when they met at the store.
   Message: _____
   Listening: _____

4. "How are you today?" asked Jed's physician when he walked into the examination room.
   Message: _____
   Listening: _____

5. "Turn left at Main Street and go straight. You can't miss it."
   Message: _____
   Listening: _____

Check Your Answers

1. On the surface, this seems to be an informational statement, but it may be the beginning of a persuasive argument. (In Chapter 5 you will learn a term for this kind of statement.) When a sales-person visits, we are usually listening in order to decide.

2. A cathartic statement! The speaker is upset. Listen empathetically.

3. A typical bonding statement to begin a conversation.

4. A different context gives a different meaning to the same words. Probably the physician is seeking information.

5. An informational statement. The listener has asked a question and is now listening to learn how to get someplace.

1

Now compose a conversation in which at least four types of communication are represented:

_____

_____

_____

_____

What types of messages did you illustrate? Keep a record of the various kinds of messages you hear during the course of a typical day. What kinds do you hear most often? Least often? Remember, each type requires a slightly different attitude and set of skills on the part of the listener. Interpreting what we hear depends in part on our ability to recognize which of the five types of communication is taking place. The chart below lists the five types of message and the corresponding modes of listening.

Purpose of Message	Listening Goal
Social	Bonding
Appreciative	Enjoying
Informational	Learning
Persuasive	Deciding
Cathartic	Enabling

It is important to be able to distinguish among these types of listening because each requires that the listener exhibit slightly different skills. A situation involving persuasion calls for a different kind of listening than a situation in which you are being entertained. Someone who is practicing critical listening will try to spot weaknesses in the speaker's argument and use of evidence. This approach, however, would be the opposite of the noncritical stance that characterizes a good empathic listener. A good listener will have the ability to recognize and practice the type of listening required in a specific situation.

1

■ A Step Beyond

Take a few moments to reflect on your own skills as a listener. Rate yourself on a scale of 1 (poor) to 5 (excellent). At which of the five types are you most adept? Least adept?

Social:	1	2	3	4	5
Appreciative:	1	2	3	4	5
Informational:	1	2	3	4	5
Persuasive:	1	2	3	4	5
Cathartic:	1	2	3	4	5

■ Looking Back

Make a list of 10 instances in which you listened to another person yesterday. How many different circumstances were involved (face-to-face conversation, a lecture, a communications medium such as the telephone or radio)? What kind of listening did the situation call for? Did the situation involve more than one kind of listening?

Situation	Type(s) of Listening
1. _____	_____
2. _____	_____
3. _____	_____
4. _____	_____
5. _____	_____
6. _____	_____
7. _____	_____
8. _____	_____
9. _____	_____
10. _____	_____

Now recall a situation in which someone demonstrated particularly effective listening skills. What type of listening was involved? What did that person do that impressed you?

_____

_____

_____

_____

Start a Listening Diary

To learn as much as possible from this book, you need to participate actively. Designate a notebook as your *personal listening diary*. Keep a list of your listening encounters. Don't try to identify every example. You will be too busy writing to listen! But do list the important examples. Identify the type(s) of message and the mode(s) of listening. Be sure to include examples of encounters where you believe you did not listen well or fully understand what you heard. This diary will provide a valuable source of examples as you complete the exercises in the rest of this book.

Chapter 1 Checkpoints

✓ Communication is the process by which one person sends a message to another.

✓ The process of communication has four elements:
    The sender
    The message
    The channel of communication
    The receiver

✓ Listening involves a sequence of four actions:
    Sensing
    Interpreting
    Evaluating
    Responding

✓ People communicate for five purposes:
    Social bonding
    Entertainment
    Information
    Persuasion
    Catharsis

✓ Different situations call for different types of listening.

✓ Different types of listening demand different skills.

2 | Giving and Getting Feedback

This chapter will help you to:

- Understand the concept of feedback.
- Distinguish among different kinds of feedback.
- Provide appropriate and productive feedback in a variety of circumstances.

Jim Washington stopped to look at the display of perfumes as he walked through the store.

"May I help you?" asked the salesperson.

"No, just looking," Jim said.

He browsed for a few moments and then walked over to the next counter.

Angela Moriarty, the salesperson at the second counter, noticed the look of combined intensity and confusion on his face. "Hello," she said, "how can I help guide you through this maze of perfumes?"

"I'm looking for a gift for my wife," he replied.

"Well," she said, "let me ask you some questions about her so you can buy just the right perfume." ■

Listening is an active process. In Chapter 1, you learned about the basic process of communication. In addition, you learned how to distinguish among various types of messages. In this chapter, we will add another element to the process of listening: the obligation of the listener to provide feedback to the speaker. We will describe what feedback is, illustrate different kinds of feedback, and help you develop the ability to provide appropriate, productive feedback in a variety of situations. The right kind of feedback can significantly improve the process of communication. The wrong kind can stop a conversation cold.

WHAT IS FEEDBACK?

Feedback refers to any message sent by the listener to the speaker either during or after the speaker's presentation. Your response to the whole message is a form of feedback, as are any messages that you send, intentionally or unintentionally, while the other person is speaking. As we mentioned earlier, it is impossible *not* to send a message to another person with our actions. This general rule applies to our actions whenever we are listening to a speaker who can see or hear us.

Think back to a recent conversation. While you were listening to the other person, how did you act? Surely you were not completely motionless. If so, the other person probably would have stopped talking to see if you were all right. Did you nod your head or otherwise indicate that you were paying attention? Express agreement or disagreement? Ask the other person to repeat something?

All these actions are examples of feedback. In any communicative situation, the listener will exhibit some form of response. That response may range from fascination to boredom, from approval to violent disagreement. This feedback may aid or hinder the process of communication. The successful listener is not only aware of the role of feedback but also able to use feedback effectively.

RETHINKING THE MODEL

We must, then, add a new dimension to the model of communication that we presented in Chapter 1. Communication, especially spoken communication, is an interactive process in which the listener can offer feedback at almost any time. The new version of our model looks like this:

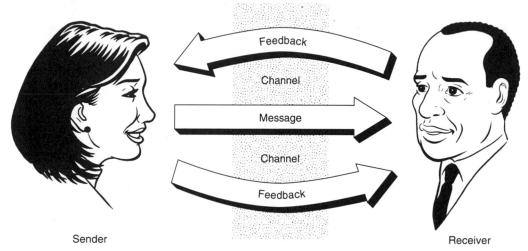

Sender

Receiver

The Communication Model with Feedback Added.

FEEDBACK WITHOUT WORDS

One of the reasons we are always giving feedback is that it does not have to be expressed in words. Applause that interrupts a speech is feedback. Laughter after a joke is feedback proving that the joke worked. Silence itself can be feedback. It can indicate that people either did not get the joke or did not like your attempt at humor.

Posture, facial expressions, and gestures are all forms of silent, nonverbal feedback. Pay attention to the physical response of another person as you speak. What is that person doing? Now think of your own behavior as others speak. Do you tend to indicate interest? Approval? Disagreement? Apathy?

Some American Assumptions

Every culture operates according to unwritten rules of behavior. Most Americans expect a listener to maintain eye contact or to look at them during a conversation. In addition, they want the listener to show some form of physical response to them. Be an observer of communication as you read this book. You will probably be surprised by the amount of physical and verbal feedback you see.

Beyond the Book

Look around you. What forms of feedback do you observe in the following situations?

1. A personal conversation.
   Physical: _____
   _____

   Verbal: _____
   _____

2. Interaction between a customer and a salesperson.
   Physical: _____
   _____

   Verbal: _____
   _____

3. Conversation between a diner and a server in a restaurant.
   Physical: _____
   _____

   Verbal: _____
   _____

Understanding Nonverbal Feedback

Nonverbal feedback is being expressed all the time, all around you. While no expression or gesture has one universal meaning, you have acquired a vocabulary of expressions just as you have a vocabulary of words. Read the following descriptions of postures, facial expressions, and actions. Write down what you think each one is likely to communicate to another person:

1. Leaning forward in chair: _____
2. Leaning back in chair, arms folded: _____
3. Resting chin in both hands: _____
4. Yawning: _____
5. Smiling: _____
6. Frowning: _____
7. Smiling and nodding: _____
8. Glancing at watch: _____
9. Looking around room: _____
10. Tapping fingers on table: _____

Possible Answers

1. Interest
2. Hostility or apprehension
3. Contemplation
4. Boredom
5. Pleasure, agreement
6. Displeasure
7. Active agreement
8. Growing disinterest
9. Losing interest
10. Impatience

2

Now stand in front of a mirror. Using just facial expressions and posture, try to indicate the following attitudes:

1. Openness to what a speaker is saying
2. Lack of interest
3. Interest
4. Antagonism, unwillingness to listen
5. Skepticism
6. Agreement
7. Worry
8. Boredom
9. Thoughtfulness
10. Intellectual excitement

Positive and Negative Postures

Although no posture or gesture has one correct or inevitable meaning, the way a person looks while listening *always* sends a message to the speaker. A good speaker will notice this feedback. Although it is not possible to know how the speaker will interpret your posture, an effective listener will tend to send positive messages of interest and concern to the speaker.

DIRECTIVE FEEDBACK

Feedback, whether verbal or nonverbal, serves two main purposes. It tells the speaker that we are listening and indicates our response to what we are hearing. Feedback that *conveys an evaluation* of what the speaker is saying is usually called *directive*. We are giving an explicit or implied value judgment about what we are hearing. A positive response expresses your satisfaction, interest, or agreement with what you are hearing. A negative response indicates displeasure or disagreement.

■ Time Out

Look back at your responses to the preceding exercise. Which of the postures and gestures you were asked to interpret would normally be considered positive? Negative?

1. _____	6. _____
2. _____	7. _____
3. _____	8. _____
4. _____	9. _____
5. _____	10. _____

■ General Rule

In general, *while someone is speaking* it is better to use directive feedback sparingly. If you do offer directive feedback, positive feedback is preferable. Negative feedback, research has shown, will cause the speaker to speak less candidly, thus robbing you of some information. The other person will appreciate signs that you are interested in what that person has to say. But it is better to hold off on indications of your critical response—whether you agree or disagree with what you are hearing—until the other person has finished speaking or has specifically asked for your appraisal.

NONDIRECTIVE FEEDBACK

When you provide feedback that either conveys no judgment (implied or explicit) or gives an ambiguous response, you are offering *nondirective* feedback. An ambiguous response is basically noncommittal. You are expressing a willingness to listen, but the speaker cannot tell whether you like what you are hearing.

Remember, feedback can be either verbal or nonverbal. Maintaining eye contact with the other person, for example, indicates without words

2

the fact that you are interested and listening attentively but does not provide clear evidence of whether you agree or disagree. When you are conversing on the telephone, you probably fill in the pauses with expressions such as "I see" or even "uh huh" to let the other person know that you are still on the line. Such nondirective response is important because it tells the speaker that you are listening.

"What I Hear You Saying Is"

A particularly valuable form of verbal feedback is *paraphrasing*, that is, restating for the speaker what you believe is the essence of what has just been said. By occasionally checking your interpretation with the speaker, you accomplish several goals. First, you demonstrate your *active interest* in the speaker. You are taking the trouble to show this speaker that you are listening. Second, you guard against the development of any serious misunderstanding. The speaker will be able to correct any minor misinterpretations before they cause problems. Third, you increase the quality of the communication by showing the speaker what information is getting across to you and what is not. The speaker can then adapt his or her presentation after taking your feedback into account.

▌ Practice Paraphrasing

For this exercise, you will need to work with another person and use a tape recorder. Find a subject on which the two of you disagree (for example, a political issue). Have the other person state his or her opinion for two minutes. You then should attempt to paraphrase the other's view, beginning with a statement such as "As I understand it, you said" or "What I heard you say was." The other person then states whether your paraphrase was accurate. Now listen to the tape recording of your conversation and discuss (1) how accurately each of you was able to paraphrase the other's remarks, and (2) what types of misunderstanding, if any, appeared.

USING QUESTIONS AS FEEDBACK

Asking questions is a specific and extremely effective way both to offer feedback and to improve the quality of communication. Whether a question gives directive or nondirective feedback depends on the way it is asked. Your language and your tone of voice let the other person know whether you are just asking for information or you are simultaneously asking for information *and* expressing your evaluation.

Threatening versus Nonthreatening Questions

A threatening question combines a request for information with some form of attack on or challenge to the speaker. It is a form of directive feedback, since you are taking the opportunity to let the speaker know that you disagree with what you are hearing.

> **Nonthreatening:** "Did you say that 50 percent of the people you polled believed candidate X?"
>
> **Threatening:** "Do you expect us to believe that 50 percent of the people you polled believed candidate X?"

A threatening question will arouse much the same response as a threatening gesture: a defensive posture.

Open versus Closed Questions

We also make a distinction between *open* and *closed* questions. Consider this question: "Do you know what a closed question is?" Your answer will be yes or no. The question was phrased in such a way that it would be difficult for you to offer a more elaborate answer. Simply put, a closed question seeks a brief answer and cuts off the opportunity for the person answering to say more than a few words. *A closed question limits the role of the person answering.*

An open question, on the other hand, attempts to evoke a longer, more complex answer. An open version of the same question would be "what

2

do you think is meant by a closed question?" This question invites a longer reply. If asked in this way, you would probably offer a definition and perhaps an example or two. *Open questions try to evoke a complex response that draws on the knowledge and experience of the person answering.*

■ Think about It

The story at the beginning of this chapter illustrates the difference between a closed and an open question. By asking a closed question, the first salesperson put Jim Washington in the position of having to answer yes or no. Many people feel awkward about asking for help, so Jim just said no. Angela Moriarty, on the other hand, eliminated his need to ask for help by asking him to describe *how* (not *if*) she could assist him. Her open question showed interest in Jim as a person.

What Kind of Question Should I Ask?

The value of a question depends on the situation. In general, closed questions are used by speakers who wish to remain in control of the situation. A lawyer in court, for example, asks closed questions. Closed questions can also be an effective means of bringing a discussion to a conclusion. A salesperson wishing to guide a customer to a decision will use closed questions as the decision to buy grows more likely.

When you are seeking information, open questions are generally preferable, since they encourage the other person to give a more detailed and personal response. The more open the question, the less likely you are to give clues to the other person concerning the answer you would like to hear.

■ **Test Yourself**

Rewrite the following closed questions so that they are open in nature:

1. Did you like the meal?

   _____

2. May I help you?

   _____

3. Are we doing all we can to promote customer satisfaction?

   _____

4. Does anyone see a flaw in our approach?

   _____

5. Have you solved the problem?

   _____

Possible answers:
1. How was the meal?
2. How may I help you?
3. In what ways can we promote customer satisfaction?
4. What is your evaluation of the strengths and weaknesses of our approach?
5. How are you addressing the problem?

Multiple Choice: A Mid-Way Approach

Sometimes an open question proves too open. What do you do if the person to whom you are talking does not respond to your open questions? In this situation, it is often useful to combine the qualities of both an open and a closed question. What kind of question is both open and closed? The multiple-choice question.

2

Consider question 3 in the exercise you just completed. You want to use a question to evoke response from someone, but that person does not know quite how to frame his or her thoughts. It might prove useful to rephrase your question to give that person some *choices* as possible foundations on which to build a more elaborate answer. "In promoting customer satisfaction, are we paying enough attention to marketing surveys, prompt response to complaints, and quality of merchandise?"

WHY ASK QUESTIONS?

People ask questions for four main reasons:

1. To seek information.

Undoubtedly you have heard someone speak about a subject that arouses your interest. Perhaps the speech increased your appetite for more information about that subject. What did you do? Probably you asked the speaker to recommend books on the subject, to elaborate on one aspect or another, perhaps even to continue the discussion at another time. While the first two types of questions are most often nondirective, questions of this sort clearly express your positive response.

Obviously, a curiosity-based question will be *nonthreatening* and *open*.

2. To check an interpretation.

In the course of a conversation or a presentation, it is useful occasionally to offer your provisional interpretation of the speaker's main points and then ask if that interpretation is accurate. Such questions serve two purposes. They express your continuing attention. They also let the speaker know whether he or she is getting the message across.

If your goal is to check your understanding, you might profitably introduce your question with a brief paraphrase of what you think the speaker has said. Then ask "Is this correct?"

Questions meant to check an interpretation are usually *closed* and should always be *nonthreatening*.

3. To clarify something.

Whenever you find yourself confused, ask questions at the first opportunity. A clarifying question asks the speaker to restate in a different way what he or she has just said. You want the other person to use not only different but also clearer and more understandable language.

A second form of clarifying question seeks additional information to support an assertion that the speaker has made. If the speaker says that "most Americans" support a particular view, you might ask the basis for that assertion (results of a poll, for example).

Questions seeking clarification should be *open* and *nonthreatening*.

4. To challenge the speaker in some way.

Sometimes it will be proper to ask questions that challenge the speaker. Perhaps you have heard statements that you believe are false or misleading. Perhaps the speaker has made a sweeping generalization. Your questions should be *open* to allow the speaker to clarify the point you are challenging. In this case your question will necessarily be *threatening*. You have to decide how threatening to make it.

Chapter 2 Checkpoints

✓ The listener is a partner in the process of communication.

✓ Feedback can enhance the quality of an interaction.

✓ Employ open, nondirective feedback to elicit more candor and information from the speaker.

✓ Paraphrase to check your level of understanding.

✓ Ask questions to evoke more information.

3 | Noise Pollution

This chapter will help you to:

- Understand the concept of noise.
- Distinguish between external and internal barriers to communication.
- Recognize attitudes that are barriers to effective listening.

"Another meeting," thinks Bob Wade, yawning. "Probably more of the same old stuff. Oh no, it's Halverson. I'm not looking forward to this."

Bob's gaze wanders around the room. "What's he going on about this time? I bet they're raising quotas again. And he'll spend the whole time trying to justify the decision."

Bob takes a sip of coffee. "I hate the way he stumbles over his words. It's hard enough to hear a good speaker over that awful buzzing from the fluorescent lights. What?"

Something catches Bob's attention. "Did he really say 'the data shows' just now? Any fool knows that *data* is a plural noun."

Bob looks to his left, annoyed, and thinks, "I wish Jones would stop tapping his pencil that way. It's really annoying. Say, that's a handsome tie he's wearing."

The presentation by his colleague has drawn to a close. Bob gets up and says to himself, "Well, this was a waste of time. I didn't hear anything new." ■

In Chapter 1, we described listening as a four-phase process that involves sensing, interpreting, evaluating, and responding. Each stage provides a necessary foundation for the effectiveness of the next.

In Chapter 2, we explored the concept of feedback and the important role that asking questions and eliciting other forms of response, verbal and nonverbal, play in the process of communication.

But despite our best efforts, often messages are not understood. Something goes wrong. This chapter will examine a concept that influences listening and may prevent us from reaching an accurate interpretation.

WHAT IS NOISE?

Since the first stage of listening involves hearing what the other person has to say, obviously we need to recognize and overcome any barriers that interfere with our hearing. After all, before we can interpret or evaluate any spoken message, we must hear it as clearly as possible. Anything that distorts or interferes with communication is called *noise*. During the first stage of listening, noise refers to factors that keep us from hearing the other person accurately. During the second stage—interpretation—noise refers to any factor that prevents us from reaching an accurate understanding of what we hear.

EXTERNAL NOISE

Some forms of noise are outside the receiver's control. External noise can come from either the environment or the speaker. An example of external noise is static on the radio that drowns out the broadcaster's words. Staring into a bright light behind the speaker can be noise if it distracts

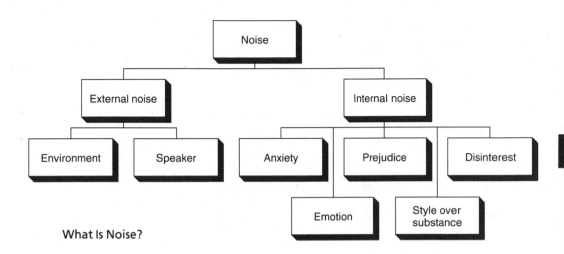

What Is Noise?

our attention and makes it difficult to concentrate on what is being said. A mannerism on the part of the speaker that annoys us and distracts us from hearing clearly is also considered noise. Mumbling, for example, is a form of external noise.

■ Time Out

Consider the story of Bob Wade at the beginning of the chapter. What external factors distracted Bob's attention?

_____

_____

■ A Step Beyond

Write down a list of problems that have distracted you or made it difficult for you to listen. We have provided two examples of speaker-related and environment-related noise to get you started. Your own list will be more useful than any we could provide.

3

Noise Related to the Speaker

Speaks too softly
_____
Doesn't finish sentences
_____

_____

_____

_____

_____

Noise Related to the Environment

Room too hot or cold
_____
Someone coughing
_____

_____

_____

_____

_____

Tuning Out External Noise

Speaker-Related Noise.   Now that you are aware of some forms of external noise that affect you, you need to act assertively. You can create an exercise that will strengthen your ability to tune out speaker-related noise. Ask a friend to help. Have that individual read a prepared speech (about two minutes long) concerning an issue related to your business. In each version of the speech, the speaker should emphasize *one* of the behaviors that you find distracting (for example, tapping a pencil or mumbling). Concentrate on *listening through* the annoying mannerism; that is, focus your attention on the content of the speech until the noise loses its power to distract.

Repeat this exercise as needed for each of the speaker-related mannerisms that you have identified as annoying. Ask your friend to record a different speech and emphasize a different mannerism each time.

Environment-Related Noise.   The most productive response to environment-related noise is to change the environment. First, examine your office and/or primary meeting rooms. Identify aspects of these places that create noise. Those that are in your power to alter change. Make a list of the others. Use your list as the basis of a meeting to discuss changes that might improve the environment for better communication.

What about Telephone Conversations?

Many people who listen well in person have trouble listening on the telephone. The most common complaint? Since the speaker is not present, listeners sometimes find themselves visually distracted. While conversing on the telephone, they look through papers on their desk, for example, or wave to people passing by.

If you are visually distracted when using the telephone, try one of the following solutions:

1. Position the telephone in such a way that you are facing away from distraction (a doorway or a window, for example).
2. Practice visualizing the individual on the other end of the connection. Speak as though that person were facing you.

You may often find it necessary to take notes while speaking on the telephone. To avoid awkward interruptions of the conversation, try this simple rule of placement. If you are right-handed, position your telephone so that you will pick it up with your left hand. If you are left-handed, position the telephone so that you will pick it up with your right hand. When you want to take notes, you will not risk losing the thread of the conversation by having to switch the telephone from one hand to the other.

INTERNAL NOISE

Other types of noise are internal. They exist within the listener and keep that individual from hearing what someone else is saying. For example, an employee who has just received a negative evaluation may be too upset

3

by that evaluation to listen closely to any suggestions for improvement. Anxiety is a form of internal noise.

Another form of internal noise is prejudice. A listener who believes that certain groups of people are untrustworthy will be likely to give a sinister interpretation to any statements made by members of those groups.

Consider Bob Wade again. What were the chances of Bob hearing anything new at the presentation? Bob's environment presents two examples of external noise: buzzing lights and the tapping of his neighbor's pencil. The speaker also has at least one mannerism (his mumbling) that distracts Bob. Notice also that Bob's attitude increases the likelihood that external factors keep him from hearing. Bob doesn't really want to hear. He is what we call a noisy listener.

Noisy Listeners

You have already learned that different situations require different kinds of listening. In general, poor listening skills can cause the noisy listener to apply inappropriate kinds of listening. For example, someone may listen critically in a situation that calls more for informational or empathic listening. Bob Wade was more interested in finding fault than in learning something new.

The following characteristics are common among ineffective listeners. They are all forms of internal noise. Find one or more examples of each form of noise in Bob Wade's behavior. Then write down any instances of your own behavior that reflect the same form of noise.

Lack of Interest.   Noisy listeners tend to prejudge the topic as uninteresting and the speaker as inept. They are listening for proof that they are right rather than being attentive to what the speaker has to say.

Bob Wade: _____

_____

Yourself: _____

_____

_____

Attention to Style over Substance.   Noisy listeners focus on the delivery rather than on the content of the message. Since they expect not to like what they hear, they are looking for distractions in the speaker's appearance or manner of presentation.

3

Bob Wade: _____

_____

Yourself: _____

_____

_____

Emphasis on Details.   Noisy listeners tend to concentrate on details rather than on the overall message of the speaker's presentation. Moreover, such listeners tend to listen for mistakes of fact made by the speaker. Listening for mistakes is often described as an *ambush* mentality.

Bob Wade: _____

_____

Yourself: _____

_____

_____

Too Much Emotion.   Noisy listeners are too sensitive to emotional issues. An emotion-laden word or concept will cause these listeners to leap to a judgment or will reinforce their tendency to regard the speaker's words with suspicion.

Bob Wade: _____

_____

Yourself: _____

_____

_____

■ One Step Beyond

Be aware of your emotional "on" buttons. Everyone has subjects or even words that arouse an immediate, strong emotional response. Below is a list of subjects. Next to each, identify the intensity level of your feeling. A 1 indicates only a mild response, while a 5 indicates an extremely strong response. Are your feelings positive or negative about this subject?

SUBJECT	LEVEL OF RESPONSE	POSITIVE	NEGATIVE
Abortion	1 2 3 4 5	☐	☐
Labor unions	1 2 3 4 5	☐	☐
Affirmative action	1 2 3 4 5	☐	☐
Censorship	1 2 3 4 5	☐	☐
Violence on television	1 2 3 4 5	☐	☐
Gun control	1 2 3 4 5	☐	☐
Universal health care	1 2 3 4 5	☐	☐
Free trade	1 2 3 4 5	☐	☐

Now record your response to the following words.

TERM	LEVEL OF RESPONSE					POSITIVE	NEGATIVE
Environmentalist	1	2	3	4	5	☐	☐
Politically correct	1	2	3	4	5	☐	☐
Republican	1	2	3	4	5	☐	☐
Liberal	1	2	3	4	5	☐	☐
Feminist	1	2	3	4	5	☐	☐
Democrat	1	2	3	4	5	☐	☐
Downsizing	1	2	3	4	5	☐	☐
Harassment	1	2	3	4	5	☐	☐
Gay	1	2	3	4	5	☐	☐
Fundamentalist	1	2	3	4	5	☐	☐

Overcoming Internal Noise

Notice that internal noises share two common qualities. Each is rooted in an *attitude* toward the speaker and the situation that makes the listener both *less likely to listen fairly* and more *susceptible to distraction* by external factors.

If you enter a situation expecting the worst, you will find it. Rather than working to ignore distractions, the noisy listener uses them as another reason to dislike a presentation.

In general, a positive attitude toward the speaker leads to more careful and thoughtful listening. Even a positive attitude, however, can hinder your ability to listen if your feelings cause you to impose your interpretation on the speaker. Every listener has prejudices (both for and against various issues) that can hinder the attempt to come to a fair interpretation and evaluation of others' statements. The issue is not whether you are affected by forms of internal noise but how well you are able to overcome them.

3

▮ Reversing the Trend

Even poor habits have their value. They can serve as guideposts to more effective behavior. This exercise is based on the assumption that each noise-creating or noise-sensitive tendency can point to a more productive mode of listening. Beside each of the following characteristics of ineffective listeners, write the *opposite* behavior.

NOISY BEHAVIOR	EFFECTIVE BEHAVIOR
Too much emotion	_____
Attention to style over content	_____
Emphasis on details	_____
Desire to ambush speaker	_____
Susceptible to emotional triggers	_____
Quick to judge	_____
Easily distracted	_____

By listing the opposite behaviors, you have described the characteristics of a listening attitude that diminish the impact of noise. Now go back to the beginning of the chapter and rewrite Bob Wade's behavior to illustrate the principles of positive, assertive listening.

_____

_____

_____

_____

_____

_____

_____

_____

_____

_____

_____

_____

_____

Chapter 3 Checkpoints

✓ The term *noise* refers to anything that interferes with or distorts a message.

✓ External noise is related to the speaker and/or the listening environment.

✓ Internal noise refers to a problem within the listener.

✓ An effective listener is aware of both forms of noise and works to control their effect.

4 | Listening to Learn

This chapter will help you to:

- Listen for content rather than style.
- Identify and remember the main points of a presentation.
- Take notes more effectively.

Matthew Lewis began the staff meeting with a story he had heard the day before.

"You have heard of Dr. Pavlov," he began, "the doctor who discovered the concept of conditioned behavior. Almost 10 years before Pavlov performed his experiments, a doctor in the United States was conducting his own research concerning reflexes. He was tapping patients just below the kneecap with that little rubber hammer that doctors still use. Well, in an article he published long before Pavlov announced his discovery, the doctor put *in a footnote* a statement that sometimes his patient would jerk his leg forward *before* he was tapped on the knee. I guess the doctor was so intent on what he was looking for that he was blind to what he could have seen." ∎

In Chapter 1 we discussed the process of listening and its role in communication. In Chapter 2 we explained various forms of feedback and their role in listening. In Chapter 3 we identified factors that can distort the listening process by preventing us from hearing or interpreting accurately what someone is saying. By developing ways to overcome these distortions, you have prepared yourself to increase your interpretative abilities. You are now ready to apply the basic principles of effective listening to specific listening situations.

The three most common types of business-related listening situations are defined in terms of the primary purpose in listening: to learn something, to decide something, or to help another person resolve something. The purpose of this and the following chapters is to help you develop a *goal-oriented* approach to listening. Each goal—to learn, to decide, to enable—calls for a different approach.

We will begin with situations where you are *listening to learn.* Receiving accurate information provides the foundation for the other forms of listening. The best decisions are based on the most complete and accurate evidence. Therefore, listening to learn is the basis of everything that follows.

LISTENING FOR INFORMATION

In the course of a typical day you will often find yourself listening primarily to receive information or to learn something from another person. What is the proper attitude for such a listening situation?

Begin with your *purpose* for listening. If your goal is to acquire information or to learn something from the speaker, then common sense should tell you that you should listen primarily to the content of what the speaker is saying. Moreover, it would be counterproductive to correct or challenge the speaker. You may win the argument, but you will not receive all the information possible.

Think about It

Ramona Childers was sitting in the back of the room, observing the performance of Cindy Goodman, the new fourth-grade teacher.

Teacher: Can anyone tell me what famous sailor was the first European to land in America?

Billy: I know!

Teacher: Yes, Billy?

Billy: Christopher Columbus done it!

Teacher: No, Billy, he *did* it.

Billy (to another student):   I could have sworn that Christopher Columbus discovered America.

Put yourself in Ramona's situation. What would you say to Cindy in discussing that particular interchange?

_____

_____

_____

_____

Note that Cindy responded to Billy's grammar instead of his answer. The correction, though fair and accurate, confused Billy, who thought the teacher was talking about the information he had just given.

How else could Cindy have responded? Write down a response that you think would be more suitable in this situation.

_____

_____

_____

_____

Perhaps a more productive response would have been to say, "That's right, Billy. It was Christopher Columbus. By the way, the grammatically correct way to state your answer would be that Christopher Columbus *did* it."

In this case, the teacher has to keep in mind the purpose of the question. Was it more important to find out the answer to a question about history or to test the use of a particular point of grammar?

FORMAL AND INFORMAL LISTENING

Listening-to-learn situations tend to fall into two broad categories: *formal* presentations, in which the listener's opportunity for active participation is limited, and *informal* situations, in which the listener has an opportunity to interact with the speaker.

Formal Listening

Formal situations include the following:

- Lectures
- Videotape presentations
- Films
- Reports at a staff meeting

In a formal listening situation, you will have no, or at best limited, opportunity to interact with the speaker. You may be able to ask questions at the conclusion or perhaps interrupt the presentation occasionally, but the speaker controls the communication process.

Informal Listening

In informal listening situations there is an opportunity to interact with the speaker. The most informal mode of communication, of course, is a *conversation*. When you are conversing with someone, you have ample opportunity to ask that person questions and make comments.

Checkup

Many situations fall between the extremes of a taped lecture and a friendly conversation. Here is a "formality" scale. Put a checkmark indicating where each example of communication falls on the scale.

	INFORMAL ⟵⟶ FORMAL
Televised demonstration	_____
Report at staff meeting	_____
Classroom lecture	_____
Receiving directions from a passerby	_____
Consultation with a physician	_____

REACHING YOUR GOAL

The desired outcome of listening is your ability to comprehend material that is being presented. You will have listened successfully, for example, if you are able to perform the task that has been described, pass an examination on the ideas that have been explained, or transmit what you have learned to others. This desired outcome—comprehending the material—should guide your listening behavior.

The goal has three main aspects:

1. Make sure that the message is getting through to you as accurately as possible.
2. Concentrate on *what* the speaker is saying rather than *how* the speaker is presenting it.
3. Try to reach an interpretation that is as close to the intended meaning as possible.

The rest of this chapter will explore listening behaviors that increase the likelihood of your comprehending the material that is being presented.

▮ T i m e   O u t

List five recent listening-to-learn situations. State the situation. Was it formal or informal? Define the *desired outcome* of that situation. Then, on a scale of 1 to 5, rate your success in reaching the desired outcome.

SITUATION	FORMAL/ INFORMAL	DESIRED OUTCOME	SUCCESS LEVEL
1. _____	_____	_____	1 2 3 4 5
2. _____	_____	_____	1 2 3 4 5
3. _____	_____	_____	1 2 3 4 5
4. _____	_____	_____	1 2 3 4 5
5. _____	_____	_____	1 2 3 4 5

4

A LEARNING ATTITUDE

When you find yourself listening to learn, it is often useful to adopt the role of a reporter or a translator. Listen as though you will be asked to paraphrase what was said or even translate its essential message into another language. When you are listening to a longer presentation, be prepared to explain the main ideas and the overall structure of the speech.

The Credibility Factor

What factors make you more or less inclined to trust the information that you hear from a particular person?

An obvious question should occur to you as (or, even better, *before*) you listen to someone offer information. Is this person qualified to speak about this subject? In other words, what are the person's *credentials?* For example, whose information about nutrition or weight loss would you take more seriously: a registered dietician, or someone demonstrating a new product?

A second factor you should consider is *experience*. Sometimes experience provides as much authority to a person's words as does formal training. For example, if you're lost in a strange part of town, the most informative person to ask will be someone who lives in that part of town.

The third factor is the speaker's *objectivity*. Occasionally you will have to take into consideration whether the person might have a bias that would make his or her information unreliable. For example, a salesperson might give you only the information that presents a product in the best possible light. A Democrat might give incomplete or biased information about the record of a Republican opponent (and vice versa!). An "infomercial" on television probably is less objective than a news report on the same subject.

Whenever possible, *prepare* to listen by doing your homework about a speaker, especially if that person is giving a lecture or other formal presentation. Your preparation should include finding out the person's credentials and discovering whether anything might bias the speaker.

4

How to Hear "This Is Important"

When you are listening to learn, concentrate on the *content* of the speaker's words. Ask yourself, is this point important? Do I need to remember this point?

Most speakers have two basic ways of telling you what parts of the explanation or the lesson are the most important.

This Is Important!   The first method is straightforward. The speaker will say, "This is important." Or the speaker will indicate that the next statement is important in another way:

1. By leaning forward.
2. By speaking more loudly or emphatically.
3. By gesturing more broadly.

How many other ways can you think of that a speaker will use to call your attention to the importance of what he or she is about to say?

_____

_____

_____

_____

Let Me Repeat . . .   The second infallible indication of importance is *repetition.* In spoken communication, unless there is a prepared text, the speaker is usually thinking through what he or she is telling you. The points that the person thinks are important will keep coming to mind. When you hear the speaker repeat certain facts or portions of the directions, focus your attention on them. The speaker is telling you that they are important.

NOTE TAKING

In formal circumstances, the key to effective listening is *disciplined note taking.* Since you will have at best a limited opportunity for feedback, it is wiser to concentrate on what the speaker is saying than on trying to give any feedback.

Note taking is one of those activites that we often take for granted. You probably took notes in school. You have most likely also taken notes at lectures and presentations and perhaps while talking on the phone. But have you ever thought about improving the efficiency and the value of your note taking?

Approaches to Note Taking

People take notes in various ways. A common approach is simply to write down everything that is said. This approach, unfortunately, leaves you with a page filled with writing that is often hard to read a few days later.

One aspect of note taking that you need to consider is making the page attractive. A messy page is like a messy desk. The clutter makes it difficult to find what you are looking for! Research has shown that the less attractive the page, the less likely you are to review your notes.

Furthermore, if everything looks about the same, you will be less likely to spot the points that struck you at the time as important. The key to effective note taking is not to record everything but to record the important aspects of a presentation *in a way that will catch your eye when you review them.*

Here are some of the most popular and effective ways to take notes.

The Outline Approach. Many people take notes in *outline* form, writing only one sentence or a few key words on each line. Others vary this approach by writing important points in large or bold letters, drawing blocks or circles around significant points, or *underlining* important statements. This approach offers the advantage of later guiding you to the elements of the presentation that you thought were particularly significant.

I. Candace's presentation on the Mackie project

  A. Deadline

    1. need to beat the competition

    2. cost vs. speed?

  B. Production method—should we handle this ourselves?

    1. in-house production group cost

    2. freelance cost? more efficient?

  C. Input from Mackie group

    1. Jerry to call them

    2. I should follow up

Notes in Outline Form.

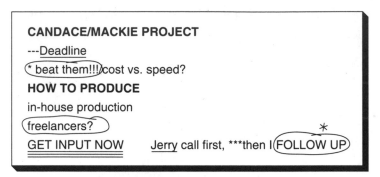

Notes Emphasized with Circles and Lines.

Clustering.   For briefer speeches, consider placing the main point (which the speaker often makes at the very beginning) in large or bold letters in the center of the page. Then write the speaker's supporting statements at various points around that center (figuratively and literally) of attention.

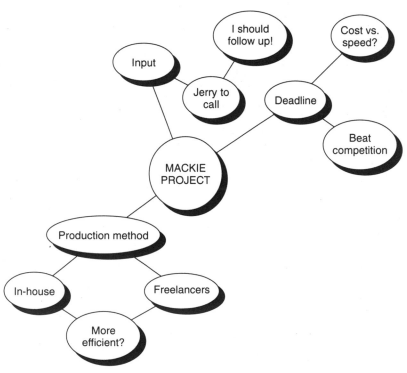

Notes in Cluster Format.

The Two-Column Approach.   Divide your notebook or sheet of paper into two columns. On the left side, enter the speaker's main points. Use the right side for specific facts (names, dates, etc.) that support or elaborate on those main points.

This approach to taking notes is extremely useful for a longer presentation. If you use this method, remember to listen for indications from the speaker that "this is important."

LISTENING IS INTERACTIVE

How much information you remember when listening to learn is up to you. While your ability to interact with someone giving a formal presentation is limited, informal listening situations will provide you the opportunity to use your feedback skills. Here are some basic response techniques that will increase the amount of information you gain from conversations and other informal situations.

Show Your Interest

Demonstrate your interest in the speaker by keeping actively involved in the conversation. Once you have determined that the speaker wants to impart information, limit your input to statements and questions that will evoke more information about the subject, repetition of information already given, or clarification of material.

Listen to Learn, Not to Win

Avoid refuting or debating with the speaker. Focus on the information level of the speaker's statements. Recall the goal-oriented approach to listening. Don't judge what you have heard in terms of its entertainment value but in terms of what you learned.

Paraphrase, Paraphrase, Paraphrase

Remember, speakers will generally indicate what parts of their information are particularly important. Listen for *emphasis* and *repetition.* Whenever the speaker gives a statement emphasis or repeats an idea, take this opportunity to practice your feedback skills. Paraphrase what you have just heard, and check your understanding with the speaker!

DO YOU LISTEN AS YOU TALK?

When you are the speaker who is *giving information,* use the techniques of feedback to make sure that the other person is receiving the message accurately. When you are the speaker in an informational situation, you have two obligations:

1. To express the information clearly.
2. To check with the person(s) to whom you are speaking to make sure that they understand the information you are presenting.

"Your little boy has an infection in his left ear," said Dr. Maxwell.

The young parents, their concern evident in their faces, stared attentively at him.

"I'm giving you an antibiotic in this bottle," he continued. "Now don't worry. Billy will be fine. I have even given you this dropper to make the application easier. Just give him four drops every two hours, and the infection should clear up in a day or two." ■

■ Stop and Think

Suppose the parents were to leave now and go home. How might they be confused about the directions given by the doctor? Why?

_____

_____

_____

It would not be surprising if the parents were unsure about *where* to administer to medicine. Should they put the drops in the infected ear? Should they give him the drops to swallow? Both procedures make sense.

It is also not unusual for the parents of a sick child to be too distraught to ask questions. Dr. Maxwell could prevent a possible crisis with one or two questions. Let's continue the situation so that the possibility of error is lessened.

4

Dr. Maxwell smiled reassuringly. "Do you understand these directions?"

"I think so," replied Billy's mom. "We should use the dropper to put the drops . . ." She paused to think. "In his ear, right, doctor?"

"I'm glad I checked with you," said Dr. Maxwell. "No, the dropper is to make the medicine easier to swallow!" ■

Review What You Have Learned

The following exercises require a partner.

1. Pretend that you are a waiter. Ask someone to place the following order:

"I would like Shrimp Scampi, a baked potato, and the green beans. About the baked potato: bring sour cream and chives on the side. I would also like a mixed green salad with Italian dressing. Bring the dressing on the side also. To drink, I will have—let me see—coffee with cream. My friend will have broiled salmon, rice and also the green beans, a spinach salad, and iced tea. She also wants the sour cream and chives on the side. We'll order dessert later."

When the other person has finished, repeat the order as accurately as possible.

2. You have stopped at a service station to ask directions:

"To get to the expressway from here? No problem. When you pull out of the station you will be on Campbell Road. Turn right on Camp-

4

bell. At the fourth traffic light, turn left. This is Alamo Road. Go north until you come to a corner with a service station on the left and a small shopping center on the right. This will be Fifteenth Street. Turn right and drive five blocks and you will reach the expressway."

Now repeat the directions.

3. A salesperson is explaining benefits of a product:

"This exercise machine imitates the action of cross-country skiing. The walking movement exercises not only your calf muscle but also the thigh muscles. Meanwhile, by moving your arms back and forth against the resistance provided by the springs to which the handles are attached, you are also working out the major muscles of your arms, especially the biceps and triceps. Of course, your cardiovascular system receives the greatest benefit because you are doing what we call aerobic exercise. Finally, notice that the machine comes equipped with an electronic device that tells you how long you have exercised and how many calories you have burned."

Answer the following questions about this presentation:

1. On what activity is the machine modeled?
2. What arm muscles are exercised?
3. Of what does the electronic device keep track?
4. What system of the body is benefitted by aerobic exercise?

Check Your Performance

In this exercise, consider your performance in two ways:

1. How much information did you remember?
2. To what degree did you employ the listening techniques discussed so far? Did you take notes? Interrupt the speaker to ask clarifying questions? Stop the speaker at least once to paraphrase or repeat the key word(s) of the presentation?

Chapter 4 Checkpoints

✓ When possible, prepare for formal listening situations.

✓ Assess the speaker's credibility.

✓ Judge content rather than delivery.

✓ Listen for ideas rather than isolated facts. Focus on key words.

✓ Develop the method of note taking that works best for you.

✓ In informal situations, paraphrase key points as often as possible.

5 | Listening to Decide

This chapter will help you to:

- Develop skills of critical listening.
- Understand the difference between an assertion and a claim.
- Distinguish between valid and manipulative forms of persuasion.
- Base decisions on the quality of arguments rather than accept assertions.

Max Niemeyer listened intently to the debate on the proposed school bond.

"Sure it will raise taxes a little," argued the first speaker, "but without the money that this bond will raise, our children will receive an inferior education. Our school district spends $11.23 less than the state average per pupil."

"That's typical talk from a tax-and-spend liberal," stated the spokesperson for the group opposing the bond. "You can't solve every problem by throwing money at it."

"You're just a reactionary, against progress," replied the other. "If we vote down this proposal, the school district will have to cancel next fall's football season. What will you say then to a fine young man like Tom Rinaldi, who needs an athletic scholarship to attend college?"

Max shook his head in dismay. This discussion was not helping him make up his mind. ■

The most common, and perhaps the most important, form of communication to which you will listen during your business career will be *persuasive* in nature. Someone will be trying to sell you something: a product, an idea, a course of action. Persuasive communication is all around you. Every day we are bombarded by a wide range of messages trying to convince us to try or buy something. Such situations call for *critical* listening.

UNDERSTAND BEFORE DECIDING

When you find yourself in a situation that requires a decision based on your assessment of what another person has said, strive for a *balanced* attitude. You are not there to refute the other person's statements, nor are you there to accept whatever you hear. You are there to discover whether the reasoning the other person is offering is useful to a decision that you are considering. Is it in your best interest to follow that person's advice?

Remember to design your *approach* to listening around your *reason* for listening. The goal of listening to a persuasive speech, above all, is to analyze the quality of the argument that you hear in order to make an informed decision.

The starting point for listening to decide, then, is the same as that for listening to learn. Your *first priority is to understand what the other person is saying.* When you are listening to decide, the nature of this understanding becomes more complicated.

ASSERTIONS AND CLAIMS

The art of persuasion has three main elements: assertions, claims, and arguments.

What Is an Assertion?

The starting point for any attempt at persuasion is the assertion. An assertion is simply a statement of opinion or fact.

"The earth is round."

"This bracelet is a good buy."

"We ought to advertise less on radio and more on television."

Each of these statements is an assertion. The speaker states a fact or an opinion without backing up the statement in any way.

An assertion by itself should not be enough to convince you. You would just be taking someone's word at face value or doing little more than responding to someone who says "Do this because I say so."

How Does an Assertion Become a Claim?

An assertion is less convincing than a *claim*. A claim is *an assertion supported by evidence*. By evidence we mean anything offered by the speaker to justify a statement. The best evidence is that which you can verify. The worst evidence is just another assertion.

Consider the three assertions given above. What kind of evidence would you expect the speaker to offer to support each?

ASSERTION	EVIDENCE
1. The earth is round.	_____
2. The bracelet is a good buy.	_____
3. We should advertise on TV.	_____

Here are some possible answers:

1. A photograph from space or a quote from any science text.
2. The price of another bracelet of comparable quality.
3. A survey of consumer behavior, or reputable studies of the effect of various advertising media on buying patterns.

Your first job, then, is to distinguish between claims and assertions. Since assertions are not supported by any evidence, you should view them with suspicion. In essence, the speaker is asking you to accept what he or she is saying on face value. Do you want to trust any person that completely?

Whenever you hear an assertion, demand evidence. If you hear a statement that is not supported by evidence, you are listening to an assertion and not an argument. Either refuse to accept the assertion or recognize the reasons for your acceptance. Are you accepting the assertion because it states an opinion most reasonable people share, because the speaker is someone whose authority you trust completely, or simply because what you hear agrees with your preconceived opinions?

Time Out

Examine the following assertions. What kind of evidence offered by the speaker would create a claim that you would find convincing?

1. This company must reorganize in order to remain competitive.

   _____

   _____

   _____

2. We should immediately implement a policy forbidding smoking in our building.

   _____

   _____

   _____

3. We should go to Italy on our vacation this year.

_____

_____

_____

FAIR PLAY OR MANIPULATION?

You learned in the preceding chapter that it is important to consider the *source* of the information that you are hearing. When the other person is trying to persuade you and the information you hear is being used as evidence, the question of credibility that we discussed in the preceding chapter becomes even more important.

The very fact that someone is trying to persuade you indicates that you will not hear an equal presentation of both sides of the issue. The other person will probably be providing only that portion of the information that fits his or her case. It is essential, therefore, to consider the speaker's credibility.

Even when the speaker cites evidence, consider the source of that evidence. For instance, the speaker may cite a recent scientific study that shows eating chocolate to be "an effective way to fight tooth decay." A study that came to this conclusion actually exists—but it is important to know that the research was sponsored by manufacturers of chocolate candy.

Arguing Fairly

Now add another element to your consideration. *How fairly does the other person try to convince you?* As an effective listener, you should focus your attention on the way the speaker uses *evidence* to support the claims he or she makes and the decision to which those claims lead you.

Your second obligation as a critical listener, once you have identified a claim, is to evaluate the quality of the evidence presented to support it.

Obviously, the most positive form of persuasion occurs when the other person uses evidence that is fair and accurate. The worst case occurs when the other person tries to manipulate you by making the evidence appear stronger than it actually is or by diverting your attention from weaknesses in the evidence.

WARNING SIGNS

In an ideal world, persuasion would always be fair. The speaker would present all the facts, even those that might weaken the overall argument, and trust you to make a wise decision. In the real world, however, people will try to lure you into a decision based on inadequate evidence. Watch out for:

Loaded Language

The easiest way to hide weaknesses in evidence is by appealing to the emotions of the listener. An effective way to lure a gullible or unwary listener to your side is to use emotionally charged language—positive terms to describe the preferred choice and negative terms to describe any alternative.

The goal of the loaded language approach is to lure you into *associating* very positive feelings with the speaker's product, or negative feelings with the opposite product.

EXAMPLES:

The defendant was lurking *near the store.*

A gang *of* punks *was* loitering *nearby.*

Someone using neutral language would say that the defendant was standing near the store or waiting there. A positively charged description would picture a group of young people chatting or even having fun.

Some speakers even preface their loaded language with a disclaimer such as "I'd be the last to bring up my competitor's troubles with the Securities and Exchange Commission". In this way, the speaker both makes the unfavorable association and can claim not to have done so! The technical name for this type of unfair argument is *praeteritio* (a Latin word meaning to go past or to overlook something).

Advertisers often call this the "spit in the beer" strategy. The speaker will say "I don't know about my competitor, but at our brewery we don't let our employees spit in the beer." What the speaker is doing, of course, is planting in your mind (without directly saying it) a negative assumption about the other brands.

The opening vignette of this chapter is teeming with examples of loaded language. Obvious examples are such terms as "tax-and-spend" and "liberal" on the one hand and "reactionary" on the other. But a verb like "throwing" (rather than "spending") money is also a way to load your language.

To make yourself less susceptible to this form of manipulation, review the sections in Chapter 3 devoted to *internal noise*. Review and expand the list of terms to which you have a strong emotional response. Loaded language, remember, can exploit your emotions two ways: it can turn you away from a positive alternative, or it can lure you into a potentially disastrous choice.

Loaded language appears not only by itself but also (often) in connection with each of the following rhetorical techniques.

The Limited Choice

Because the speaker knows that you are listening for the purpose of making a decision, he or she often will try to "help" you by defining the terms of the choice for you. Unfortunately, that definition makes only one of the choices attractive. The key phrase that should cause your internal warning lights to flash is *either . . . or.*

A situation presented as an either-or dichotomy may be oversimplified. The speaker may be excluding a wide range of alternatives in order to limit your choice to an unappealing option versus the option the speaker is trying to persuade you to make. When given an either-or choice, make an effort to think of the options that have been omitted.

EXAMPLES:

The choice is clear. We have to initiate the proposed changes or lose our competitive advantage.

Mom, all the other kids are going. If you don't let me go too it means that you don't love me.

Either we pass this bond or we will have to cancel the football season.

The Stacked Deck

The stacked deck is a cousin of the limited choice. In this case, the speaker presents only one side of a complicated argument. This technique will provide the listener with a profusion but not a range of evidence. If an alternative is mentioned, the evidence cited about it will be negative. The effective listener will ask whether there is another side to the relentlessly positive or negative picture presented by the speaker.

EXAMPLE:

We should give lie detector tests to all prospective employees. The tests will screen out possible bad risks. Anyone who refuses to take the test undoubtedly has something to hide. And of course these tests are now 90 percent accurate.

COUNTER-EXAMPLE:

We should not give lie detector tests to prospective employees. Those tests are are wrong at least 10 percent of the time, so we could ruin someone's reputation for no reason. Besides, some people whom we really want could refuse to take the test on principle. We appear to be prying into their personal lives.

In both examples, the speaker is giving only one side of the argument. Now you might well ask: Why should anyone offer evidence against the position that he or she is arguing? Think about it. Research has shown that we are *more* likely to be convinced if we believe that the person has tried to present the other side of the picture. While we can't expect someone to present all the evidence against his or her position, we should be concerned when we hear none.

The Sweeping Generalization

Among the words that should inspire skepticism in the effective listener are *all, every, none, never,* and *always*. Every statement that makes a sweeping generalization is potentially manipulative (including the sentence you are reading now). In general, it is advisable to be wary of assertions that cover whole classes of people, ideas, or situations. What kind of evidence, after all, could the speaker offer that would support such a statement?

EXAMPLES:

All politicians are crooks. You can't trust anything they say.

Nobody over 40 listens to rock music.

I'm merely expressing what everyone thinks.

Everyone else is going!

A common variation on the sweeping generality is the *bandwagon* suggestion. The speaker states or implies that "all your customers" or "the people who matter" agree with the statements or are rushing to buy the product.

If you challenge a sweeping generalization by pointing out an exception, don't let the speaker get away with the rejoinder that "the exception proves the rule." This adage is actually a misinterpretation of an old Latin saying (one that makes much more sense, by the way) that the exception *dis*proves the rule. The word *proves* (from the Latin *probare*) meant "to challenge" centuries ago when the saying was coined, but its meaning has changed over the years.

The Anecdote

Speakers who want to gain your sympathy will often describe in detail the plight of a specific individual. To convince you to adopt an investment strategy, they may recount at length the success of one or two people who followed their advice. Using a specific case in this way is the corollary of the sweeping generalization. The assertive listener will wonder if there are cases out there of people whose stories would counter the one offered by the speaker.

EXAMPLES:

> *American education is pathetic. I read in the newspaper about a student who graduated from high school and couldn't read.*

> *If the bond doesn't pass, young Tom Rinaldi won't be able to go to college. And he is one terrific young fellow.*

Coincidence as Cause

"The last two companies to switch to our service," notes the speaker, "saw their profits rise by more than 10 percent."

This assertion implies that the rise in profits was caused by the use of the new service. The effective listener, however, will spot this misuse of evidence as confusion between coincidence and cause. Just because A happens after B, it does not mean that A was caused by B.

EXAMPLE:

> *The universities are teaching anti-family values. My ex-wife went back to school to get her degree and left me six months later.*

There might be other reasons why she left him! Remember, the speaker who is trying to persuade you will often leave out pertinent information.

Each of the forms of persuasion described above might be described as a case of "the weaker the argument, the louder the voice." People often raise their voices or wave their fists to divert you from the flaws in their arguments. Similarly, a speaker who lacks strong evidence or an argument that will convince the careful listener will seek to divert you. Arousing your emotions clouds your ability to notice that there is no real evidence. If there is hidden evidence, you can't see all the possibilities.

THE STRUCTURE OF PERSUASION

Sometimes a well-formulated claim will be enough to convince you. But one claim, even a strong one, is rarely enough to convince anybody. Most of the time the other person will use a variety of assertions and claims. Just stringing a few claims together won't be very effective. An attempt to persuade you, especially a formal presentation such as a speech, will have a *structure* designed to lead you into accepting the speaker's recommendation. Usually the other person will need to weave together a series of claims to make a case strong enough for you to say, "Okay, I agree." A series of claims woven together to make the point is an *argument.*

There are three main ways to structure an argument.

Persuasion by Example

In this approach the speaker will organize a sequence of examples or facts that lead the listener to a natural or obvious conclusion. The speaker purposefully holds back the main point until the end, in the hope that the listener will see that point before it is made. We call this form of argument *induction,* from the Latin verb *inducere* (to lead into), because the speaker leads the listener to a conclusion.

Problem–Solution

This is the most straightforward way to structure an argument. It has three main parts. First, the speaker *identifies a problem.* The speaker then *proposes a solution* to this problem. Finally, the speaker presents facts and arguments to show the wisdom of the proposed solution.

EXAMPLES:

> *Unemployment is endangering the economic health of our nation. I would like to suggest some reasons for this problem and propose a plan to overcome them.*

> *We have had numerous complaints from our customers concerning the speed—or rather, the snail's pace—of our deliveries. After studying this problem, I believe that I have found some bottlenecks and discovered ways to speed our process of getting the product to our valued customers.*

Five-Step Motivational Approach

Have you ever attended a speech that began with a joke and ended with a call to action? Did the speaker invite you to imagine the improvements in your company or your life if you adopted the course of action that was being proposed? If so, you were probably listening to someone with formal training in the art of public speaking.

Many professional speech writers use a structure of persuasive speech that is based on a sequence of five principles: attention, need, solution, visualization, and action. This five-step approach is an expansion of the problem–solution structure.

1. The speaker begins by *grabbing the listener's attention,* usually with a joke or clever story. This beginning is also called a *hook.*
2. Next, the speaker takes advantage of the listener's attentiveness by *identifying the problem* that the speech will address.
3. In the third part of the speech, the speaker proposes one or more possible solutions to this problem.
4. The fourth part of the speech is the key to its power. The speaker describes the positive results of adopting the proposed solution. The speaker often invites the audience to *"visualize along with me"* this happier future: how much more succesful the company will be, or how you will be happier (thinner, more popular) as a result of following the speaker's advice.

5. Finally, now that the audience is on the speaker's side and inspired by this visualization, the speaker will conclude with a set of specific actions to take and a *rousing call to action.*

■ Time Out

Identify the rhetorical technique(s) in each of the following examples.

1. This health care proposal is nothing more than socialized medicine.
2. I will take the high road in this debate. I won't mention my opponent's problems with the IRS.
3. Think of the advantages of the new design. The car will have a more efficient aerodynamic design, use less gas, and be more attractive.
4. But, Mom, all the other kids are going!
5. The alternative to hiring this applicant is a law suit.

REMEMBER: THE LISTENER DECIDES

This chapter has emphasized unfair forms of argument to keep you from making decisions you will regret later. When you notice that the speaker is relying more on emotions than on reason, or more on trickery than on evidence, adopt a defensive listening posture.

If possible, ask the speaker questions until you are satisfied that you have enough evidence on which to base your decision. If you can't ask questions directly, delay your decision until you can examine the validity of the evidence and the fairness of the argument.

Chapter 5 Checkpoints

Critical listening is an essential skill. Remember to begin by envisioning the most productive outcome: the best decision based on the best evidence.

✓ DON'T:

Be manipulated. Know your weak points and guard against their exploitation.

Accept assertions.

✓ DO:

Seek to *understand.* Base your decision on the validity of the various claims and the overall structure of the argument.

Discover the speaker's *method of argument* and use of evidence.

Spot manipulative techniques.

Ask questions until you are satisfied.

6 | Listening to Enable

- **This chapter will help you to:**
- Recognize situations that require empathic listening.
- Create an affirming listening environment.
- Understand and endorse feelings expressed by others.
- Lead others to devise solutions to problems.

Tom's Dilemma

Ed Martin had asked to speak with his supervisor. When he entered the office, Ed seemed agitated. His jaw was clenched, and he was perspiring.

Tom Carlton looked at his obviously troubled employee. Getting up from his seat behind his desk, Tom motioned Ed to sit on the small sofa and pulled up a chair so he could sit facing him.

"I'm getting sick and tired of busting my tail for this company when nobody seems to care," Ed said, his voice quavering with indignation.

"Well," Tom thought as he looked at Ed. "What do I say now?" ∎

WHAT IS EMPATHY?

As you learned in Chapter 1, empathy is the ability to imagine another person's point of view, to project yourself into another person's situation in an effort to understand his or her thoughts *and feelings.*

Empathic listening has much in common with listening for information. Both seek understanding rather than assessment. Both demand thoughtful, intelligent attention to the speaker.

Empathic listening, however, differs in two important ways from other forms of listening.

Listening to Feelings

First, empathic listening addresses the emotions as well as the ideas of another person. In addition to understanding the information that another person is conveying, the empathic listener is trying to imagine the feelings that lie behind the statements and even to imagine the world from the speaker's perspective.

In Chapter 5, we cautioned you to beware of people who consciously try to manipulate your emotions. In this chapter we will help you respond to people who are genuinely expressing their own emotions.

A Different Focus

Second, empathic listening has a different focus than other forms of listening. Whether listening for information or listening to decide, your focus is on yourself. *You* want to understand. *You* have to make a decision.

When listening empathically, you want to *enable the other person.* The good of the other person is your main concern. Can you help that person understand the reason for the feelings being expressed and get past those feelings to act on what is causing them?

Focus on Drama.   A situation that calls for empathic listening usually is initiated by a *dramatic* occurrence, most often a *problem*.

- A coworker asks for help in coping with a troublesome colleague, in performing a frustrating task more effectively, or in adjusting to a bothersome change in the work environment.
- A customer complains about a service, product, or employee.
- A friend or family member wants to talk about a personal dilemma.

Focus on Emotions.   Situations that call for empathic listening are also marked by *strong emotions*. The speaker will express strong emotions such as joy, anger, or dismay.

- A coworker may be visibly upset.
- A customer may be angry enough to shout or cause an unpleasant scene.
- A friend or family member may burst into tears.

EMOTIONS EQUAL MESSAGES

"That personnel appraisal was unfair and untrue!"

"You hate me!"

"This is the worst day of my life!"

What do you do when you hear a statement filled with strong emotion? Your immediate goal as an empathic listener is to see the situation as the other person sees it. Only then can you help that person deal with those emotions.

Remember, the other person's feelings are not an obstacle to the message; these emotions *are the message*.

TWO BIG DON'TS

1. Don't Judge

The first and foremost caution for the empathic listener is this: *Don't judge.*

When we are upset (or angry or happy or in love), the last thing we want to hear is "you shouldn't feel that way." (How would you respond if you were upset and someone told you it was ridiculous to be angry?) Such a statement implies that the other person thinks we are not worth talking to!

2. Don't Advise

Your job is not to propose a solution but to help the other person create his or her own solution. People are more likely to act on a course of action in which they have a personal investment. This feeling of investment results from playing an active role in coming up with the particular course of action.

KEEP YOUR GOAL IN MIND

As in the previous chapters, approach listening from the analogy of "form follows function." First, decide the *best* and *worst* possible outcomes of a specific situation; then plan to act in a way most likely to promote the desired result.

Consider the conversation between Ed Martin and his supervisor. The worst outcome might be that Ed leaves the office not only with the problem unresolved but also with the feeling that Tom is an uncaring or incompetent manager.

The best outcome would be that Ed leaves the office thinking that Tom cares about his problem, that there was nothing wrong with feeling the way that he did, and (best of all) that he believes he is able to come up with a useful response to the situation that upset him in the first place.

What should Tom say to promote the best rather than the worst result?

AFFIRM, UNDERSTAND, ENDORSE, ENABLE

There are four goals of empathic listening. You will not necessarily accomplish them in the order given here, but keep all four in mind.

1. *Affirm* the legitimacy of the speaker's feelings.
2. *Understand* the situation from the speaker's perspective.
3. *Endorse* the importance of both the speaker and the issue.
4. *Enable* the speaker to find a resolution to that problem.

Be aware that if you *don't* reach these goals, you will damage, if not destroy, your effectiveness as a listener. Remember:

The opposite of affirmation is disinterest.

The opposite of understanding is assumption.

The opposite of endorsement is disqualification.

The opposite of enabling is hindering.

Goal 1: Create an Affirming Environment

When someone comes to you with a problem, you have an opportunity to affirm the feelings and the person. Affirming means simply indicating that it is OK to have these feelings. The other person is not bad or foolish to have these feelings.

The key element of such affirmative listening is the environment in which the conversation takes place. This environment includes both the physical setting and the attitude of the listener. How can you create an environment in which the other person is more likely to speak candidly and you are more likely to listen attentively?

Open the Lines of Communication.   To create an affirmative environment for open communication you must respond to the other individual *as a person.* Minimize authority. Find ways to indicate your concern for the speaker as a human being rather than as an employee or as a customer or any other role.

It is usually best to deal with emotional issues in a more private setting. The possibility that others will overhear will make some people reticent to speak their minds. Other people might respond to an audience by becoming even more dramatic. If the conversation occurs in your office, make that setting as friendly as possible.

■ Your Turn

In his conversation with Ed Martin, what steps did Tom Carlton take to create an affirming environment?

_____

_____

_____

_____

Did you notice? As soon as he realized that Ed was upset, Tom tried to minimize the difference in status and power separating the two of them. Since a desk is a symbol of authority, Tom moved from behind it.

Goal 2: Understand the Problem

Having created an atmosphere in which the other person feels comfortable, you and the speaker can focus on the problem or issue that is causing the strong emotional response. Remember, your goal is to allow the other person to express his or her feelings fully. The kind of *feedback* that you offer the speaker should also be nondirective, nonjudging, and nonthreatening.

Since your goal is to discover the speaker's view of a problem, you will find two kinds of feedback most useful:

1. Paraphrasing.   Repeating the main points that the speaker has made is particularly useful early in the conversation. You are asserting your intention to get to the heart of the matter and are showing your interest in the other person.

Empathic listening involves a greater range of paraphrasing than do other forms of listening. Your goal is to understand the feelings of another person, and these feelings are often difficult for the other person to express. Look for:

   a. Surface meaning (key words).
   b. Underlying emotion.

2. Clarifying.   Since the emotional state of people with strong concerns often makes it difficult for them to state their views clearly, the ability to ask clarifying questions takes on added importance. Indeed, the alert listener in an empathic situation will hear some (perhaps all) of the rhetorical strategies discussed in Chapter 5. The difference is that the statements are more likely to reflect the speaker's inner turmoil rather than a deliberate attempt to manipulate you.

Goal 3: Endorse Importance

In empathic listening, it's not enough to understand the nature of the other person's emotions. You have to show the speaker that:

   1. He or she is important to you.
   2. You want to understand the situation.

Use your *feedback* skills to endorse the importance of the other person.

- Lean forward.
- Make eye contact.
- Use expressions such as "I see" and "Go on" to indicate that you are indeed paying attention.

Disinterest Disqualifies.   Remember the rule of communication: You can't *not* communicate! Be aware that a person with a problem is more likely to read things negatively. It might surprise you to learn how easy it is to send (even unintentionally) a negative message that other people will interpret as an indication that you do not care.

Don't:

- Look at your watch.
- Let your eyes wander.
- Ask the person to get to the point with words or gestures that express impatience.

Your Turn

Practice writing *affirming* responses to the following statements:

1. Customer: "I can't get anyone to respond to my problem."

   _____

   _____

   _____

2. Customer: "One of your salespeople was rude to me when I tried to return this."

   _____

   _____

   _____

3. Employee: "I want a transfer. My supervisor is making my life miserable."

_____

_____

_____

Suggested Responses

In each case you want to make the speaker aware that you understand both the problem and the feelings (frustration, for example) caused by the problem. You also want to lead the speaker to a conversation about resolving the problem.

1. (The customer is annoyed.) "I can understand how annoying that can be. I want to know exactly what happened. What is the problem?"

2. (The customer feels slighted and unimportant.) "Would you like me to help you with the return? After we see about the return, I'll want to know what was done to disturb you."

3. (The employee is worried about a negative evaluation.) "You sound really frustrated. Come on into my office. It's tough enough to do a job without feeling miserable."

Goal 4: Enable and Resolve

In many cases, understanding is a valuable and satisfactory conclusion to an empathic listening situation. If the other person leaves the conversation believing that the complaint was not trivial, you have _endorsed_ that person's sense of importance. By helping the other person define a problem, you may have also given that person the confidence to find a resolution for it.

The conversation may turn toward a solution of the issue. If the speaker seems ready to seek a resolution of the problem, your role as listener shifts. Your previous concern has been to enable the speaker to move from an emotional to a rational consideration of the issue. Now you want to enable that person to come up with an effective course of action.

This transition can often be effected by a *summarizing* statement. Review for the other person the conversation as you understand it. Remember to check often to make sure that the other person agrees that your account is accurate.

If the other person is willing, ask for (but don't offer!) at least one suggestion to improve the situation. You want the other person to leave thinking about that solution and the possibility of others.

LISTENING TO EMOTIONS

Two emotions that you are likely to encounter are *anger* and *despair*. These powerful emotional states also hinder us from thinking clearly. To get to the heart of the reasons for someone's anger, you must wait until the emotions have subsided.

Let Anger Run Down

Anger is a counter-productive emotion. Observe an angry person sometime. You will see how much energy that person is expending either to express the anger (shouting, stomping around) or to keep from expressing it (lips tightly pressed together, a face often flushed with the effort to keep from exploding). That effort will cause any angry person eventually to run down the way a windup toy will run down or a car will run out of gas.

Dealing with Temper Tantrums

Some people have even learned to use anger as a method of getting what they want. They are practicing the adult version of a temper tantrum! Since we are often uncomfortable in the presence of strong emotion, we are tempted to give in to someone expressing anger.

But, by giving in, we are preventing the other person both from finding a solution to a specific problem and from developing a more productive mode of behavior.

The basic rule for dealing with anger is this: Don't flinch. Listen to the anger. Validate the emotion. But above all, let the angry person's anger-based energy run down before you try to find out what is causing it.

And Let Tears Dry Up

The same basic principle should guide your response to sadness. As long as the other person is crying, he or she won't be able to listen to you. Be patient. When the tears stop falling, then practice what you have learned in this chapter.

Emotion *Can* Be Positive

So far we have discussed negative emotions, such as frustration and anger, that tend to drain energy away from more productive behavior. But not all emotional outbursts are counterproductive. What about emotional states such as enthusiasm or excitement?

Don't Open an Umbrella in a Brainstorm

When a person shows these emotions, you don't want to let the emotions run down. Show the other person that you share the excitement.

Suppose someone comes to you with an idea that has him or her electric with excitement. In this situation, the person wants encouragement, not analysis or criticism. By accepting and nurturing the speaker's excitement, you just might make the idea better!

USING YOUR KNOWLEDGE

Let's return now to the case at the beginning of this chapter. We have seen some responses that could aid Tom's goal to understand Ed's problem and help Ed find a solution.

"Ed, you're a valued member of the team here, and I'd like to know what is bothering you. If something specific has brought you here, I'd appreciate knowing exactly what it is."

Tom hopes that Ed will read this response as an endorsement of his right to feel angry as well as an invitation to expand on it.

Ed is likely now to take the conversation in one of two directions. Either he will give expression to more feelings (especially if he has been storing up resentment for a long time), or he will articulate, as best he can, the specifics of his situation.

Ask for Details

Why have we emphasized asking for *details* and *specific examples* so much? By getting the other person to concentrate on details, you help put the focus on the reasons for that person's emotions rather than on the emotions themselves. You can make the feelings a gateway to the underlying concern.

More Anger . . .

If Ed still needs to vent his feelings, remember the point made earlier in this chapter: *let him run down*. Then try again to turn the conversation to the cause of his anger.

Or Some Specific Reasons

"You know why I'm angry. I just found out that Sarah Thompson received a promotion. I've been here longer, and I'm as good an engineer as she is, maybe better."

Now Tom can deal with the issue because he knows exactly what it is. He can direct Ed's attention to his performance as an engineer.

■ Be Creative

Put yourself in Ed Martin's role. You have expressed your frustration. Urged on by Tom, you have revealed your jealousy of another person's promotion. By asking you specific questions, he has made you realize why you were passed over: You are a good engineer, but your colleagues find you aloof.

If this were the case, list some changes that you could make in your behavior that could help you get promoted the next time.

_____

_____

_____

Won't you leave Tom's office with a more confident attitude?

6

■ Your Turn

Describe a positive reponse to the following situation:

1. A coworker shows up late for a meeting, furious because he received a traffic ticket while hurrying to the appointment.

   _____

   _____

   _____

   _____

   Let him express his anger. He won't be any good at the meeting if that anger is using up all his energy. If possible, go off with him to a private setting for a few minutes.

2. You are a team leader, and a team member rushes into your office excited by a breakthrough in her research.

   _____

   _____

   _____

   _____

Try to calm your colleague down only enough to understand what she has to say. Often people excited by an idea can be led to even more interesting connections. Expressions such as "Go on!" are all you need. Do *not* point out possible problems in her idea! There will be time to deal with difficulties later, and you may keep her from making bold leaps in her thinking.

A FINAL NOTE

You might recall that we began this exploration of listening skills with an analogy to driving skills. We have guided you through the twists and turns of the road to more effective listening and even pointed out the location of an occasional pothole.

By now you are aware that listening, like driving, requires both attention and caution on the main roads and by-ways, as well as flexibility to adapt to unexpected changes in conditions.

Remember: the key to effective listening is to identify your primary goal and then to apply the appropriate techniques and skills to reach your goal.

Bon voyage!

Chapter 6 Checkpoints

✓ The skills of empathic listening are related to the goals of the listener.

✓ Whether in a personal or a business setting, your first goal is to allow the other person to express his or her feelings as clearly and candidly as possible.

✓ Work with people to find a solution to the situation that has aroused emotions.

✓ Enable people to move from feelings to positive action.

Post-Test

Test your mastery of the material in *Effective Listening* by choosing the best answers to the following questions.

1. What percentage of most people's working day is spent listening?
   a. 30%
   b. 100%
   c. 50%
   d. 75%

2. The correct order of the four phases of the listening process is:
   a. Interpret, evaluate, respond, sense.
   b. Evaluate, sense, respond, interpret.
   c. Respond, sense, interpret, evaluate.
   d. Sense, interpret, evaluate, respond.

3. Feedback is:
   a. A message sent by a listener to a speaker during or after the speaker's presentation.
   b. The vibrating sound created by an amplified instrument.
   c. An attempt by the listener to put a speaker at ease.
   d. An attempt by the listener to catch a speaker off guard.

4. To paraphrase effectively, a listener should:
   a. Repeat the speaker's words exactly.
   b. Restate the essence of the speaker's message.
   c. State his or her opinion of the speaker's message.
   d. Translate the speaker's message into industry jargon.

5. Which of the following is an example of a closed question?

   a. Why are you interested in improving your listening skills?

   b. Does the course begin on Thursday?

   c. Can you tell me a bit about your last project?

   d. How do you feel about the course beginning on Thursday?

6. In terms of effective listening, one example of internal noise is:

   a. Prejudice.

   b. Peristalsis.

   c. Feedback.

   d. Karma.

7. Listeners are cued in to important information when the speaker:

   a. Clears his or her throat.

   b. Dims the lights in an auditorium setting.

   c. Tells you something is important and repeats it.

   d. Moves quickly from topic to topic.

8. As a listener, it is more important to

   a. Judge content rather than delivery.

   b. Judge voice tone rather than appearance.

   c. Judge appearance rather than credentials.

   d. Judge delivery rather than credentials.

9. The best definition of a claim is:

   a. Evidence supported by an assertion.

   b. An assertion supported by hearsay.

   c. A measured response to a verbal attack.

   d. An assertion supported by evidence.

10. When a listener practices empathic listening, he or she:

   a. Reprimands and constructively criticizes the speaker.

   b. Withholds all response.

   c. Takes into account the emotions and ideas of the speaker.

   d. Nods repeatedly, and remains silent.

ANSWER KEY

1. *c* 2. *d* 3. *a* 4. *b* 5. *b* 6. *a* 7. *c*

8. *a* 9. *d* 10. *c*

Business Skills Express Series

This growing series of books addresses a broad range of key business skills and topics to meet the needs of employees, human resource departments, and training consultants.

To obtain information about these and other Business Skills Express books, please call Irwin Professional Publishing toll free at 1-800-634-3966.

Effective Performance Management
ISBN   1-55623-867-3

Hiring the Best
ISBN   1-55623-865-7

Writing that Works
ISBN   1-55623-856-8

Customer Service Excellence
ISBN   1-55623-969-6

Writing for Business Results
ISBN   1-55623-854-1

Powerful Presentation Skills
ISBN   1-55623-870-3

Meetings that Work
ISBN   1-55623-866-5

Effective Teamwork
ISBN   1-55623-880-0

Time Management
ISBN   1-55623-888-6

Assertiveness Skills
ISBN   1-55623-857-6

Motivation at Work
ISBN   1-55623-868-1

Overcoming Anxiety at Work
ISBN   1-55623-869-X

Positive Politics at Work
ISBN   1-55623-879-7

Telephone Skills at Work
ISBN   1-55623-858-4

Managing Conflict at Work
ISBN   1-55623-890-8

The New Supervisor: Skills for Success
ISBN   1-55623-762-6

The *Americans with Disabilities Act*: What Supervisors Need to Know
ISBN   1-55623-889-4

Managing the Demands of Work and Home
ISBN   0-7863-0221-6

Effective Listening Skills
ISBN   0-7863-0102-4

Goal Management at Work
ISBN   0-7863-0225-9

Positive Attitudes at Work
ISBN   0-7863-0100-8

Supervising the Difficult Employee
ISBN   0-7863-0219-4

Cultural Diversity in the Workplace
ISBN   0-7863-0125-2

Managing Change in the Workplace
ISBN   0-7863-0162-7

Negotiating for Business Results
ISBN   0-7863-0114-7

Practical Business Communication
ISBN   0-7863-0227-5

High Performance Speaking
ISBN   0-7863-0222-4

Delegation Skills
ISBN   0-7863-0105-9

Coaching Skills: A Guide for Supervisors
ISBN   0-7863-0220-8

Customer Service and the Telephone
ISBN   0-7863-0224-0

Creativity at Work
ISBN   0-7863-0223-2

Effective Interpersonal Relationships
ISBN   0-7863-0255-0

The Participative Leader
ISBN   0-7863-0252-6

Building Customer Loyalty
ISBN   0-7863-0253-4

Getting and Staying Organized
ISBN   0-7863-0254-2

Total Quality Selling
ISBN   0-7863-0324-7

Business Etiquette
ISBN   0-7863-0323-9

Empowering Employees
ISBN   0-7863-0314-X

Training Skills for Supervisors
ISBN   0-7863-0313-1

Moving Meetings
ISBN   0-7863-0333-6

Multicultural Customer Service
ISBN   0-7863-0332-8